POWER BASICS OF
FOOTBALL

POWER BASICS OF
FOOTBALL

James Bryce
Bill Polick

Prentice-Hall, Inc.
Englewood Cliffs, New Jersey

Prentice-Hall International, Inc., *London*
Prentice-Hall of Australia, Pty. Ltd., *Sydney*
Prentice-Hall Canada Inc., *Toronto*
Prentice Hall of India Private Ltd., *New Delhi*
Prentice-Hall of Japan, Inc., *Tokyo*
Prentice-Hall of Southeast Asia Pte. Ltd., *Singapore*
Whitehall Books, Ltd., *Wellington, New Zealand*
Editora Prentice-Hall do Brasil, Ltda., *Rio de Janeiro*
Prentice-Hall Hispanoamericana, S. A., *Mexico*

© 1985 by
James Bryce
Bill Polick

Library of Congress Cataloging in Publication Data

Bryce, James,
    Power basics of football.

    Summary: Well-known athletes and coaches present the fundamentals of
football. Also includes a history of the game.
    1. Football—Juvenile literature. [1. Football] I. Polick, Bill.   II. Title.
GV950.7.B79 1985   796.332'2   84-22838

ISBN 0-13-688318-4

Printed in the United States of America

The Early Beginnings

It is often said that the sight of falling leaves and the soft coolness that suddenly appears in the air indicate that autumn has arrived. In North America, however, the falling of leaves is a very minor sign of autumn compared to the other sights and sounds that signal the change in seasons.

It is the sound of cheering crowds and the crunching of shoulder pads that let Americans know that autumn has arrived...and so has the football season. Whether high school, college, or professional, the fever of gridiron action puts football way out front in any season. At present in the United States, football is fast becoming a sport that one day may be played in almost every month of the year.

In history (almost three thousand years of it), you can find references to some form of football being played by people the world over. The early Chinese, the Japanese, and even some ancient civilizations that are no longer around, such as the Aztecs, had a type of football game.

One story has it that in the eleventh century in England, two young men were digging for roots along a river bank when they discovered a skull that had once been attached to a man's body. The skull, bleached white by river sand and sun, was thought to have once belonged to a Danish warrior who was part of a conquering horde long driven from English shores.

Dislike for the conquerors, however, still ran rather high in "merry olde England" and the two young Englishmen decided to show their dislike by kicking the skull down the main street of their village. Other young men joined in, and soon a "game" began to form.

It wasn't long before sides, or teams, were formed (usually village against village), and a rather unsophisticated and often quite brutal game of football emerged.

5

As rough and as unregulated as it was, this game of football soon became the rage of England, and although people put their lives in jeopardy when they played the game, almost every person longed for the chance to play.

Of course, the game, or sport, that finally emerged when rules were introduced was that of soccer, as we call it here, or football, as it is still called in England and in most of the world.

Even in those early days, soccer was almost entirely a kicking game. Some schools allowed stopping the ball in flight with the hands or swatting it back with the forearm and fist, but that was the limit.

However different the rules were in the various schools, kicking the ball to advance it down the field was the basic method of play used everywhere. No one was permitted (as one written rule stated) "to run with the ball in his grasp toward the opposite goal." This rule was firm. For countless generations no one ever thought of violating it.

But the day came when the rule was broken. It was a sparkling November day in 1823—a momentous day, which eventually led to the birth of American football.

It happened at the Rugby school playing field. About one hundred players divided into two sides had been kicking the ball back and forth most of the afternoon with neither side making a goal. It was close to sundown, the time when all games were to end. The stroke of the five o'clock bell was the signal that brought the game to a close.

Just before the first stroke sounded, one side made a final attempt to score by booting the ball far and high down the field. A young man by the name of William Webb Ellis was waiting with outstretched arms for the ball to come down. He caught it, but, instead of dropping the ball and then taking a kick as everyone thought he would do, Ellis impulsively tucked the ball under his arms and—horrors—started running with it right through the enemy's ranks.

For a moment the entire side stood stunned and motionless. Then as the players realized the enormity of Ellis' deed, they made for him and tried to stop him. Angry players reached out for him, but Ellis, exhilarated by the touch of madness that had seized him, eluded them by dodging, sidestepping, and warding them off by thrusting his free hand into their faces and, yes, he crossed the goal line.

Ellis was no instant hero. Indeed, he was criticized by many Rugby school players for his flagrant violation of the rules. But he had started something. Some of the players began to realize that running with the ball was more exciting than just kicking it. They tried the new play in their informal games, and before long it was accepted and became a feature of the kind of football played at Rugby school.

Other schools heard about "that play they use at Rugby" and tried it out on their own fields. The players seemed to like the new way of playing the game, which soon became known as rugby football, or rugger. This did not mean, however, that the old kicking game was abandoned. Many athletes preferred the original game which, they maintained, was truly football in its purest form.

So with the help of William Webb Ellis, the game of rugby came into being, and two sports were then actively pursued: rugby and soccer.

Football was brought to America by the early English colonists, and the same rough-and-tumble type of game was played in this country as had been played in England.

It was not until 1862 that the sport finally became a "team" effort, with rules that set out what the game was about. The responsibility for the formation of the first football team is credited to Gerrat Smith Miller; his team was called the Oneida Football Club of Boston. The Oneida Club adopted the play of English football (or soccer), and so the first organized football team in the United States took the field in 1863.

By the early 1870s, intercollege games between schools such as Columbia, Princeton, and Rutgers were being played, and it appeared that the game of soccer had taken a firm grip on colleges and universities in the United States. The only holdout was Harvard.

It was Harvard that decided to introduce a new rule to the game of soccer. The rule was simple: "Under certain conditions a player would be permitted to grab the ball, hold on to it, and run with it."

"Impossible!" shouted the other schools. "We won't hear of

such a change," and they didn't. They refused to allow the new running rule. So Harvard did what it had to do; it kept the rule in and the other teams out.

Today in the United States, the great game of football owes its very existence to those fine Harvard students who in the 1870s held out for their special brand of football and who did not give in to the pressures of the soccer purists from the other schools.

In the ensuing years, football grew in popularity and, unfortunately, in its degree of violence. By the early 1900s, there were so many deaths and permanent injuries attributed to the game that President Theodore Roosevelt threatened to legislate against the game unless it changed its ways.

The turning point came in 1906 when the country's leading football delegates met and adopted new rules that would open up the game and forever change the complexity of the sport. The four major changes were (1) Establishing a neutral zone the length of the ball between opposing lines; (2) increasing the yardage required for a first down from five to ten yards; (3) reducing game time from seventy to sixty minutes and having a half time; and probably the most important ruling of all, (4) legalizing the forward pass, which totally opened up the game.

In John Mosedale's book *Football* (World Publishing, 1972), the author indicates that it was not only a rules change about passing that did so much but also the fact that certain teams did so much with it.

Not until 1913 did the forward pass attract national attention and at last convince the Eastern Schools that it was here to stay. The convincer was Notre Dame's upset victory over Army at West Point, gained largely by passes thrown by quarterback Gus Dorais to Knute Rockne and to other receivers. The fleet-footed Rockne was captain and left end of the Irish eleven.

The game was played on November 1, 1913, and was the first meeting of the two schools. The Irish were held lightly by Army, at that time an Eastern power on a par with the Big Three. The Cadets looked upon the game as a friendly warm-up for their annual battle with Navy. Admission was free, as for all football games at West Point in those days, and only three thousand spectators sat in the wooden stands.

Army did not know that both Rockne and Dorais, a skinny 145-pounder, had spent the previous summer practicing forward passing on the beach at Cedar Point, on Lake Erie, where they worked as restaurant checkers. For hours every day, Gus threw the ball from all angles to Knute, who ran along the beach, dodging imaginary pursuers. By the end of the summer, they were a smooth-working, coordinated pair.

Jesse Harper, Notre Dame's coach, watched them perform in the early practice session that fall and told them that they were going to be of great value to the team. The Irish eleven that took the field against Army was big and fast, and it centered around the accurate bulletlike passing of Gus Dorais.

Lightning did not strike immediately, but the first quarter was not very far along when Gus on third down suddenly shot a twenty-yard pass diagonally across the field to Knute, who took the ball over his shoulder and coasted to the goal line.

The third quarter was a standoff, but in the final quarter Dorais opened up and passed Army dizzy. His targets were Rockne; left halfback Joe Pliska; and Fred Gushurst, the right end. He got to them at distances from five yards up to forty yards and completely confounded Army's defense. Cleverly he mixed his passing attack with line smahes and end runs. The Irish made three touchdowns in the last quarter, all of them the result of passes, and won the game, 35–13.

Football writer Harry Cross reported the game in the *New York Times* and wrote that "Army's style of old-fashioned, close, line-smashing play was no match for the spectacular and highly perfected attack of the Indiana collegians....Football men marveled at this startling display of open football."

Coaches and football observers in the East also marveled at Notre Dame's performance when they read about it the next day. Many sat down with pencil and paper and began diagraming new forward pass patterns, but it took time and tedious work to develop a pass attack, and it required highly skilled players to execute it. The change did not come overnight, but the Irish had pointed the way.

Indeed, football in the United States had come of age. The brute force tactics of a fist in the face gave way to clever pass patterns and unique backfield wizardry. Coaches and players alike began to understand that balance and a good pair of hands for receiving a pass meant every bit as much as brawn.

The Cast

George Allen

Andrew Gissinger

Eric Sievers

Tom Ramsey

GEORGE ALLEN

George Allen has been one of pro football's best. He was an assistant coach with the Chicago Bears, head coach of the Los Angeles Rams, and head coach of the Washington Redskins. He led the Rams to two division championships and led the Redskins to Super Bowl VII. He is now head coach of the USFL Arizona Wranglers. With over twenty years of professional coaching experience, he has a record of success that few coaches can match.

ANDREW GISSINGER

Andrew Gissinger is a 280-pound starting lineman for the NFL San Diego Chargers. He played football at Syracuse University, where he was chosen to the 1980 All-East team. As a former dean's list student, he combines intelligence with his tremendous physical strength. These qualities have allowed him to survive in the trenches of the NFL.

ERIC SIEVERS

Eric Sievers is a starting tight end for the NFL San Diego Chargers. In his first year, he was selected to the UPI NFL All-Rookie team. Prior to this, he won letters for four years at the University of Maryland, where he appeared in six college bowl games. Eric has a habit of making clutch catches in tight game situations.

TOM RAMSEY

Tom Ramsey was honored as PAC-10 coplayer of the year while playing football at UCLA. He was an All-American selection and was honored as the Most Valuable Player in the 1983 Rose Bowl game. Tom is now quarterbacking as a professional in the United States Football League.

Contents

POWER BASICS OF
FOOTBALL

1

The Receiver

Eric Sievers

Football means a lot to me and to others who play it, but you have to realize that it is not the last thing on earth.

The people who are the most successful in the game may not always be the stars, but rather they are the ones who know that someday football will end.

I thank God that I got my college education; I stayed in school and did the very best I could, gave it my all. But I know that when my playing days are over, I will need more than just football experience, so I get a job in the off-season so I can learn other skills that will carry me through the rest of my life.

chapter 1

Conditioning

Coach George Allen
Before you can become a good receiver, you have to know the basics of catching the ball. That takes hand-eye coordination, and there are some special drills you can use to develop the skill.

PRACTICE THE BASICS

Eric Sievers

One of the things I like to do best in a football game is to catch the ball (Picture 1). I know that when I receive a pass, I

Picture 1

am helping my team move up the field into better field position.

There are several drills I like to teach that you can do at home, at school, or on the field in the off-season as well as during the season. Get a friend to work with you.

DRILL #1

Eric Sievers

The first drill you should try takes two players. Move six or seven yards apart, as in Picture 2. One of you is the thrower,

Picture 2

the other is the receiver. The receiver turns his back, and the thrower yells "Ball!" and the receiver turns quickly to catch the ball. The receiver should be in a good football position with legs shoulder-width apart, weight balanced, knees bent slightly, back straight, and hands up, as in Picture 3. The idea is to get used to turning quickly and picking up the ball. Be sure to throw the ball to various spots.

Picture 3

DRILL #2

Eric Sievers

The second drill begins with two players standing about five feet apart, as in Picture 4. Face each other in a good football position. Pass the ball back and forth in various locations. Do this as quickly as possible. Be sure to watch the ball all the way into your hands, as in Picture 5.

Picture 4

Picture 5

DRILL #3

Eric Sievers

For the third drill, you might want to get on some soft grass, or on floor mats if you are indoors. The receiver gets down on his knees, as in Picture 6, and the thrower lobs the ball just within reach. The receiver reaches out and catches the ball. Be sure to use both hands to catch the ball, as in Picture 7.

Picture 6

Picture 7

Picture 8

Once you catch the ball, tuck it away quickly and roll onto your shoulder, as in Picture 8. Don't keep your arms extended when you hit the ground because you might injure yourself.

chapter 2

Running the Pattern

Coach George Allen
Running the pattern means, quite simply, getting where you have to be when you are supposed to be there.

AVOIDING THE DEFENDER

Eric Sievers

There are many things that make a good receiver: good hands, speed, and good timing on a route. The key to running a successful route, however, is getting down the field and avoiding the defensive back.

Picture 9

When you are running down the field, you want to run as fast, and in as straight a line, as you can (Picture 9). When you get up to the defender, you want to make him think that you are going to do one thing, but then do another. When you are going to run a post pattern or a corner pattern, you should be right on the defensive back when you make the break, as in Picture 10. If you move too early, the back will be able to see

Picture 10

what you are doing and have time to react. You want to get your opponent moving backward and at an angle. You may not be the faster player, but if you can get the defender moving the wrong way, you can get into the open. Even if you can make great catches, you will never get the ball if you are not open. When you reach the defender, make a hard step right at him and then move off to the side. Make a hard step and then cut in the opposite direction.

DRILLS YOU CAN DO

Eric Sievers

When you are in your stance at the line of scrimmage, you want to be as low and as hard off the ball as possible, as in Picture 11. Never stand straight up, because the defender will jam you and push you back. Practice leaning forward and almost falling forward, and you will develop the right move.

Picture 11

THE SPEED ROUTE

Eric Sievers

Another route you will use often in a game is called the speed route. That is when you are going to do an outside curl or outside pattern to the flat.

In this route you run at the defensive back, but instead of chopping your step, you continue with a fluid move without breaking stride (Picture 12). The key is to throw your arm across your body in the direction you are going, as in Picture 13. That brings your hips and shoulders around and gets you moving in the proper direction.

All these moves take practice, so work on them whenever you can.

Picture 12

Picture 13

chapter 3

Coming off the Line

Coach George Allen
The first step in receiving comes when you leave the line of
scrimmage. It is not as simple as just running down the field.
You must also deal with defensive players who don't want
you to get where you want to go.

TECHNIQUES FOR THE GETAWAY

Eric Sievers

One of the biggest problems a tight end has getting off the
line is the linebacker. Linebackers are usually big and fast. But
you can beat them if you know how.

First get into a good three-point stance. Make sure your
weight is balanced so that you can go in either direction
(Picture 14). Remember that this does not give the defender any
hint of the direction you will go.

When the ball is snapped, take a hard first step in the
direction you are going, and on the second step throw your
arm across your body, as in Picture 15. If the linebacker is
trying to push you down, he will not be able to control you;
your momentum will carry you away from him. Once you have
moved past the defender, get up and run your route.

THE JUKE STEP

Eric Sievers

The next move I like to use coming off the line is called the
juke step. As the ball is snapped, fake the defender with a step
in one direction, as in Picture 16. Then cut back the other way.

Picture 14

Picture 15

As you go the other way, throw the linebacker off with your arm, and throw the opposite arm over his head, as in Picture 17. This is called the arm-over move. The fake step gets the linebacker leaning in the wrong direction, and then you can push him out of the way with your other arm, as in Picture 18.

Picture 16

Picture 17

Picture 18

FAKE BLOCK

Eric Sievers

The last release is good for running a short route to the inside or outside, a nice, quick goal line pattern or a short yardage play. It comes from a blocking move.

Try to make the defender think you are going to block him, as in Picture 19. This gets him coming at you, fighting you. When the ball is snapped, step into the defender with a good blocking technique, take a few steps, and then roll out away from him, as in Pictures 20 and 21. Be sure to keep your arms low so that you are not called for a pushing penalty.

Picture 19

Picture 20

Picture 21

chapter 4

Knowing Your Position

Coach George Allen
It is very important for you to know what you are supposed to do on the play. Don't worry about what your buddy is going to do. Concentrate on what you have to do and where you have to go.

HUDDLE THINKING

Eric Sievers

As the play is called in the huddle, I think about what play is being called, and what I have to do (Picture 22). I have

Picture 22

Picture 23

Picture 24

practiced this play many times, and when I get the snap count, I go to the line and take a peek at where the player is who will be covering me, and I check to see how the defensive zone is being set up (Picture 23).

When I am on the line, I don't worry about how my teammates will get where they are going, but I do think about where they will be. If I see that the primary receiver is going to be covered by the defense, I know that I have to be even more alert so that I can get in the open to catch the ball (Picture 24). That is also what you should do.

chapter 5

Catching the Ball

Coach George Allen
To be a good receiver, you have to know how to catch the ball. That sounds simple enough, but there is a lot more to it.

CONCENTRATION

Eric Sievers

The thing you need to work on in catching the ball is concentration. That is what catching is. Get off the line, run your route, and then think about catching the ball.

Once you catch the ball, bring it into your body as quickly as possible (Picture 25). Tuck it in and go. Try to get your finger over the nose of the ball, as in Picture 26, so that you have a good grip on it.

HAND POSITIONS

Remember that good receivers catch the ball with their hands, not their bodies. They also watch the ball all the way into their hands, as in Picture 27. If the ball is thrown over your head, get your thumbs together, bring it down, and tuck it away.

Eric Sievers

To catch the ball well, you have to get your hands in the right position. On low throws, get your palms open and put your little fingers together, as in Picture 28. Always look the ball

Picture 26

Picture 25

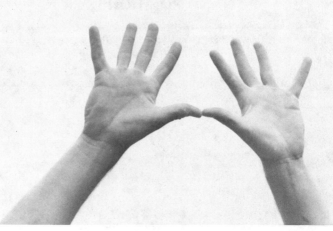

Picture 27

in; never look away. Don't worry about where your defender is until after you catch the ball.

On balls thrown right at your chest, get your hands up in front of you and out just a bit so that if the ball goes through your hands, or is bobbled, you have a chance to recover. Look at Picture 29, and you can see the proper position.

Picture 28

Picture 29

If the ball is thrown over your shoulder, put your little fingers together and form a basket, as in Picture 30.

One thing you don't want to do after you catch the ball is tuck it into the upfield arm. That is where the defender will hit you, and the ball could pop loose. Always put the ball in the downfield arm (the one toward the quarterback) for protection, as in Picture 31.

Picture 30

Picture 31

chapter 6

A Special Power Basic

Eric Sievers

One of the techniques we use for faking out our defender is called a three-step break.

As the ball is snapped, come off the line and run straight up the field—then veer off toward your defender. Take three steps to convince him that you are going in that direction and on the third step, break in the opposite direction. Not only will you have the defender moving backward, but you will also have him moving away from the direction you will be going. This should put you in the open and ready to catch a pass.

chapter 7

A Power Basics Checklist

Hand-eye coordination drills

Players move six or seven yards apart, thrower yells "Ball!", receiver turns to catch.

Players stand about five feet apart, underhand toss quickly.

Receiver on knees, dive for ball, catch two-handed, tuck, and roll.

Running the pattern

Fake your opponents by stepping one way, then going the other.

Be low and hard off the line of scrimmage.

On speed route, don't chop steps; throw arm across body for turn.

Coming off the line

To get off the line against linebacker, take hard step, throw arm across body.

For juke step, fake step one way, then go the other. Arm over defender's head and push him out of the way with other arm.

Fake block, then roll away.

Knowing your position

Know the play.

Know your route.

Watch defense.

Catching the ball

Concentration is the key.

Once you catch ball, tuck it and go.

Get finger over nose of ball.

Tuck ball in downfield arm.

Keep hands together; make a basket for the ball.

2

The Lineman

Andrew Gissinger

Playing the offensive line in football doesn't bring a lot of glory, but the self-satisfaction of successfully blocking for a touchdown, of protecting your teammates, is a lot like life in general.

There is not a lot of glory in what most of us do every day, but there is a lot of work, discipline, and fun.

If you have fun playing football, the work and discipline will not seem so bad and will prepare you for the world after the game.

chapter 8

Weight Training

Coach George Allen
Playing in the trenches requires a lot of strength and stamina. One way to develop strength is through the selective use of weight training.

BENCH PRESSES

Andrew Gissinger

I want to stress the importance of weight training with the supervision of your coach. Have your coach help you with your technique. With that in mind, there are several lifts you should work on.

There are two types of bench presses that you should use: One is a normal bench press, which is a thumbs-out grip, and the other is the close-grip press, which helps the muscles you use for pass blocking.

One thing you have to remember when you bench press is an upper body lift (Picture 32). Don't arch your back. To begin, sit on the bench and plant yourself, as in Picture 33, then lie back in a comfortable position. Hold the weights so that the thumbs are about shoulder-width apart, as in Picture 34. Lower the weight to your chest, as in Picture 35, then push it back slowly, as in Picture 36. Try to do four sets of five. This is the best for football because it will develop both strength and stamina. Remember to lift with your upper body only—your lower body is just for balance.

Picture 32

Picture 33

Picture 34

Picture 35

Picture 36

PASS BLOCKING PRESS

Andrew Gissinger

When you are allowed to use your hands to push an opponent in a game, you have to have strength—and to develop the right muscles, you use a close-grip lift. This develops exploding strength. You start as just described, but you lift your legs off the ground and cross them in the air once you have the weight, as in Picture 37. In the thumbs-out grip, you let the weight down slowly, but in this one it comes down quickly and then you explode up. When you lower the weight, it should come on to your shoulders.

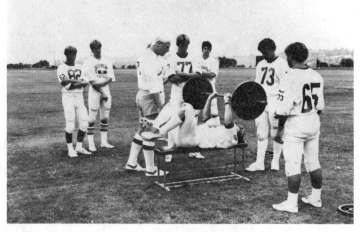

Picture 37

NECK PRESS

Andrew Gissinger

To work on developing your shoulders, you do what are called neck presses. Take the weight down behind your head so that it sits on the ridge of your shoulders, as in Picture 38, then push it up, as in Picture 39. I recommend using a weight

Picture 38

Picture 39

Picture 40

Picture 41

belt for this lift. Remember to keep your head up and your back straight. Do sets of five because this is a power lift. As soon as you do a set, pick up a set of dumbbells and lift them sideways over your head. Stand up with your feet wide and lean over slightly to isolate your shoulders. Start with your hands together and low, as in Picture 40, then bring them up and twist your wrists, as in Picture 41, and then take them back to the starting position. You should do sets of five or eight for the best conditioning.

Always remember to train with your coach's supervision.

chapter 9

The Stance

Coach George Allen
To play the line properly, you have to start by getting into the right stance. Jim Symington, head football coach at Gross-mont College in El Cajon, California, explains how to play in the trenches.

THE BASIC STANCE

Jim Symington

The fundamental stance used in football is called the three-point stance. That means both feet and one hand touch the ground. This stance, as in Picture 42, gives you the ability to move in any direction, while the four-point stance, with two hands on the ground, limits you to moving forward.

Picture 42

POSITIONING YOURSELF

Jim Symington

To get into the stance, place your feet about shoulder-width apart, then drop one foot back so that the toe is about even with the heel of your other foot, as in Picture 43. Bring the hand that is on the same side of your body as the back foot down to the ground for balance. You should stand a little pigeon-toed, with your heels a little farther apart than your toes.

Picture 43

BALANCED DECEPTION

Jim Symington

You have to be balanced so that the defender cannot tell what you are going to do. Don't point your toe or knee out or put too much weight on your hand because you limit your movement. You should be able to lift your hand and stay in position without falling over, as in Picture 44. Look straight ahead so that you keep the defender guessing.

Picture 44

chapter 10

The Drive Block

Coach George Allen
When you work in the trenches, your main job is going to be blocking. The first basic block to learn is called drive block.

THINKING AHEAD

Jim Symington

Before you ever get out of the huddle, you should know what play is going to be run, what your assignment is, and what the snap count is. When you get to the line, the only thing you need to think about is the type of block you must execute.

The time to learn your assignment is in practice, not in the game. If you don't know what you are supposed to do on a particular play, ask the coach.

THE BASIC BLOCK

Jim Symington

Blocking starts with a good three-point stance. Your eyes should be looking at the chin of your defender. When the ball is snapped, your job is to put your face mask in the defender's numbers and put your helmet right under his chin. As you come off the line of scrimmage, take both hands, as in Picture 45, and make fists and drive them right into the defender's ribs, as in Picture 46. Your knees should be slightly bent so that you are driving up to get the defender to stand up straight. Do this and you are under control. If you are the one standing straight

63

Picture 45

Picture 46

Picture 47

up, you are not controlling the play. Look at Picture 47 for a good example of a drive block.

Be sure to keep your feet moving as you block and push the defender farther than he wants to go. If you are extremely successful, the defender will end up on the ground with you on top.

chapter **11**

The Power Block

Coach George Allen
As an offensive lineman, you will sometimes find yourself
working with the man next to you to double-team an oppo-
nent. This takes practice and teamwork.

TWO-ON-ONE

Jim Symington

The power block is used in a variety of situations, but for purposes of illustration, we will use one example: the play is a power off tackle, and the offensive guard and tight end must block the defensive tackle.

The offensive tackle uses the regular drive block, as in Picture 48. As he is hitting the defensive tackle, the tight end

Picture 48

67

steps with the inside leg to drive the defensive player as far back behind the line as possible and toward the center of the field as in Picture 49. Ideally you would like to drive the defensive tackle all the way to the inside linebacker spot so that he cannot get into the play. There are variations, of course.

Picture 49

TWO-ON-TWO

Jim Symington

What happens in the example just described if the defensive tackle decides to move to the inside, as indicated in Diagram 1, instead of moving to the outside? In this situation the tight end has to be alert because a linebacker may move to the outside, and the tight end has to make an adjustment. That

offensive tackle hole. The offensive tackle stays with the defensive tackle, and both offensive linemen use the drive block, as in Picture 51.

Since you never know what the defense is going to do, you always have to be alert. The only way to really learn to do the two-on-one and the two-on-two well is to practice.

Picture 51

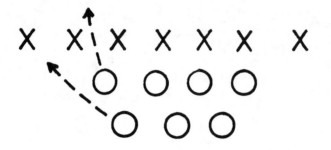

DEFENSE TACK
MOVE INSIDE

Diagram 1

is when you run what I call the doodad. When the tig
realizes that the defensive tackle is leaving him, as in
50, he is going to pick up the linebacker. He moves upfie
one more step to get his man so that he cannot make i

Picture 50

chapter 12

The Pass Block

Coach George Allen
The forward pass is a major part of the game of football today, and it is the responsibility of the offensive lineman to protect the quarterback.

THE POSITION

Jim Symington

Pass blocking starts from the three-point stance, as Andrew Gissinger is demonstrating in Picture 52. When the ball is snapped, you must get into a good blocking position with your

Picture 52

Picture 53

knees bent, hips down, hands up in front of you, as in Picture
53. Keep your feet moving.

MAKING THE BLOCK

Jim Symington

Just as the defender begins to make contact with you, take
a step forward and hit him in the chest, as in Picture 54, and
then drop back a step or so, as in Picture 55. You repeat this
action as long as you can. Set up, hit, recoil.

Picture 54

Picture 55

When pass blocking, it is important to keep your body between the defender and the quarterback. If you don't, the defender will be able to get around you and rush the passer.

Make sure to keep your elbows in close to your body, as in Picture 56. If your elbows are out, the defender will grab your arm and push you out of the play and get to the quarterback.

Be sure to use your legs and hips to drive, and hit with the heels of your hands.

Picture 56

chapter 13

A Special Power Basic

Andrew Gissinger

What I would like to mention is a play we use on the San Diego Chargers for pass blocking. It is called the quick-set.

Because we throw the ball fairly quickly, we, on the line, have to block the rushers in a hurry. We start in the three-point stance, but instead of stepping back first and setting up the normal pass block, we have our hands open and a little wider apart than normal, and we bring our back foot even with the front foot. This all happens pretty fast so that we get the advantage over the defense.

chapter 14

A Power Basics Checklist

The stance

Three-point stance: two feet, one hand on ground.
Feet shoulder-width apart, back toe even with front heel.
Heels farther apart than toes.
Hand is for balance, not support.

The drive block

Start with three-point stance.
Eyes looking at defender's chin.
Face mask in defender's numbers, helmet under his chin.
Fists in defender's ribs.
Knees bent to drive defender up and back.
Keep feet moving.

The power block

Offensive tackle uses drive block.
Tight end steps with inside leg to drive defender inside.
Doodad means tackle takes on tackle; tight end picks up
    linebacker.

The pass block

Start with three-point stance.
Set up with knees bent, hips down, hands up.
Step forward and hit defender in chest with heels of
    hands.
Step back for set-up.
Stay between quarterback and defender.

3

The Quarterback

Tom Ramsey

The game of football has been very rewarding for me, not only from the people I've been able to meet but also from being able to play with a lot of great players.

I think football builds character; it brings out leadership skills, and it teaches camaraderie. When you win, you win as a team, and when you lose, you lose together.

Being part of a team means making friends and having a lot of fun.

chapter 15

Formations

Coach George Allen

One of the essentials of playing quarterback is knowing the playbook thoroughly and knowing how much the entire team depends on you. You carry a little extra burden on the team because you have to know not only your assignment but also the assignments of others as well. Your teammates look to you as the leader.

THE "I" FORMATION

Tom Ramsey

A well-pepared quarterback knows the playbook very well and has no trouble calling the plays in the huddle or calling an audible at the line of scrimmage (Picture 57).

There are three basic formations. The first basic formation

Picture 57

is called the "I" formation. In this formation the fullback and tailback line up directly behind the quarterback, as in Diagram 2. This is basically a running formation, but you can throw play-action passes off it from time to time to disguise the pass.

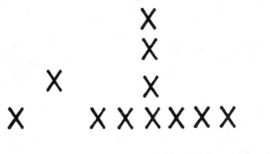

"I" FORMATION

Diagram 2

THE SPLIT-BACK

Tom Ramsey

The second basic formation is called the split-back. In this formation the fullback and tailback line up behind the offensive tackles, as in Diagram 3. This is basically a passing formation, but you can also use running plays from it.

"SPLIT BACK" FORMATION

Diagram 3

THE SPREAD

Tom Ramsey

The third basic formation is the spread. This is a single back formation, with either the fullback or tailback near the quarterback, as in Diagram 4. This is primarily a passing formation, with two receivers on each side and one blocking back.

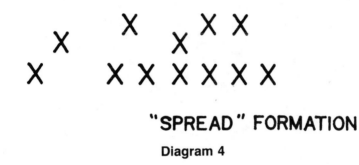

"SPREAD" FORMATION

Diagram 4

Most offensive plays come from these three basic formations, so it is very important that you become familiar with them.

chapter 16

Taking the Snap

Coach George Allen
Since almost every play in football begins with the snap of
the ball, the quarterback has to know how to get the ball from
the center. It takes timing and practice.

HAND POSITION

Tom Ramsey

The most important part of a snap is the quarterback's
hand position. To start, step up behind the center and anchor
your top hand on the center's rear end and mold the thumbs of
both hands together to make a large basket for the center to hit
as in Picture 58.

THE TRANSFER

Tom Ramsey

The center should bring the ball up and almost skip it off
the quarterback's top hand. This will push the hands apart
slightly, as in Picture 59. This leads to a natural grip.

At this point, the quarterback is not concerned about
where the laces are.

Remember to keep your hand in place until you get the
ball. Don't pull away too soon, and don't step back too soon.
Make sure you have the ball (Picture 60).

Picture 58

Picture 59

Picture 60

Picture 61

VARYING THE CADENCE

Tom Ramsey

In order to confuse the defense, it is a good idea to vary the cadence. You can have the ball snapped on various commands, emphasize different words, or vary the rhythm in an effort to draw the defense off sides (Picture 61).

chapter 17

The Drop Back

Coach George Allen
When you are in a passing situation, you have to know how to drop back and get into position to throw.

GETTING BACK

Tom Ramsey

Once you have the snap from the center, your goal in a passing situation is to get as much depth as possible. There are two ways of doing that: the five-step drop, as in Picture 62, and

Picture 62

Picture 63

the backpedal, as in Picture 63. The latter method gives you more vision across the field but is not as quick.

When you drop back on the five-step drop, the first three steps are for depth, the last two are for control. On the first three steps, get as deep as possible, with long steps, as in Picture 64. Steps four and five are shorter, as in Picture 65. On the fifth step, you should plant your foot to drive forward and stride and throw the ball (Picture 66) with a good follow-through, as in Picture 67.

Picture 64

Picture 65

Picture 66

Picture 67

FINDING THE RECEIVER

Tom Ramsey

On most plays you will have a primary, secondary, and third receiver. I like to teach what I call sequencing in picking the person to whom you will throw. Look first for the primary receiver, and if he is covered, look to the secondary receiver as in Picture 68. If that person is covered, then go to the next possible receiver.

Picture 68

Be sure to keep your feet moving while you are looking for your receivers.

A quarterback has to drive back in order to give the receivers a chance to run their patterns and to give himself the opportunity to find an open receiver and get the ball to him.

chapter 18

Passing

Coach George Allen
One of the most glamorous aspects of playing quarterback is
passing. Generally you are able to eat up large chunks of the
field with a single accurate throw, and that puts you in a
better position to score and pumps up the emotions of your
teammates.

HOLDING THE BALL

Tom Ramsey

In order to make accurate passes, you have to know how to hold the ball. Be sure to get two fingers on the laces at all times, as in Picture 69, and keep a good strong grip on the football. The fingers on the laces help you throw a spiral.

When you are holding the ball, be sure to have a gap between the ball and your palm. Don't have the ball flat against the hand because it will cause the ball to spiral down, and you won't get the proper loft on the ball. For the proper position, look at Picture 70. Keep two hands on the ball as in Picture 71, and keep the ball near your ear for a quicker release as in Picture 72.

THROWING THE BALL

Tom Ramsey

Throwing the football uses the same motion as throwing any object, such as a rock, a baseball, and so on (Picture 73).

Picture 69

Picture 70

Picture 71

Picture 72

Picture 73

Picture 74

Be sure to use a quick release. Pull your arm back, throw the ball, and follow through. The follow-through should be almost like a baseball pitch; your back leg comes through as the ball is thrown. If you don't follow through, the ball won't go as far or as accurately. As you follow through, your hand should almost be pointing at your target (Picture 74).

chapter 19

The Handoff

Coach George Allen
In order to get the maximum effect from the offensive team,
you have to vary the plays, using both passing and running.
In order to run efficiently, you have to know how to hand off
the ball.

HANDING OFF

Tom Ramsey

There are three basic types of running plays: the keeper, the pitch, and the handoff.

On all three of the plays, take the snap and bring the ball in close to your body, as in Picture 75, and turn either way. The ball should be secure and hidden from the defense.

When you hand off, be a magician with the ball. Put one hand out to give the ball to the running back but keep your other hand in your midsection to fake opponents, as in Picture 76. Be sure to place the ball firmly in the runner's stomach. You can also use a fake pass to throw the opponents off.

Make sure you have only one hand on the ball when you hand off, as in Picture 77.

THE PITCH

Tom Ramsey

On the sweep play, take the ball from the center, reverse pivot, as in Picture 78, pitch the ball to the running back, and fake the defense by pretending you still have the ball. Make sure you lead the runner with the pitch, as in Picture 79. Use a

Picture 75

Picture 76

Picture 77

Picture 78

dead ball pitch; don't put any spin on the ball because that makes it too hard for the running back to hold on to.

Picture 79

KEEPER

Tom Ramsey

The quarterback keeper play is a good move to keep the defense off balance. Once you take the snap from the center, turn and fake a handoff to the running back, as in Picture 80. Then follow the running back with your eyes, as in Picture 81. Keep the ball and go in the opposite direction of the running back, in Picture 82.

The key to the success of the play is making a good fake, hiding the ball, and following the running back with your eyes. Be sure to put the ball in your downfield arm.

Picture 80

Picture 81

Don't let the defense know where the ball is on running plays. Keep them guessing.

Picture 82

chapter 20

A Special Power Basic

Tom Ramsey

In order to develop my skill as a passer, I like to work on a throwing drill.

I get a receiver to stand about fifteen or twenty yards away and yell "Throw!" in different cadences, and I throw on his command. This helps quicken the arm and gain strength.

I also think it is important to jump rope because it develops stamina and is great for the cardiovascular system.

chapter 21

A Power Basics Checklist

Formations

Know the playbook.

The "I" formation has the fullback and tailback directly behind the quarterback.

The split-back has the backs behind the offensive tackles.

The spread has one back near quarterback and two receivers on each side.

Taking the snap

Anchor top hand, mold thumbs, heels of hands together.

Hands should separate slightly when ball is caught.

Vary the cadence.

The drop back

Five-step drop: first three steps for depth; four and five for control.

Backpedal gives better view upfield.

Look for receivers.

Passing

Two fingers on laces, firm grip.

Gap between ball and palm.

Two hands on ball while dropping back.

Ball near ear during drop.

Cock arm, throw, follow through.

The handoff

Bring ball in close to body.
Hide ball from defense.
Use fakes.
Lead the runner with the pitch.
Follow running back with eyes and keep ball.

Epilogue

Football, as played in the United States, has become a game of skill balanced with a player's physical capabilities. A bright mind coupled with quick reflexes can sometimes secure a young man's place on a team, even though he may not be the biggest, fastest, or strongest person for a particular position.

Every young person wanting to play in competitive sports must have a solid background in the basics of his sport and must learn from those beginnings so that he may continue to improve. Only by continuing to strive above those basic learning lessons will he arrive at a position he feels is secure for him, for his playing position, and for his teammates.

It might be said that the game of life is played in much the same fashion.

SOURCES

A *Hall of Fame Book, Football*
   by John Mosedale
   World Publishing, 1972

Football
   By Earl Schenck Miers
   Grosset & Dunlap, 1972

Inside Defensive Football
   by Dick Butkus
   Henry Regnery, 1972